JOHN NEWBERY

and the Story of the Newbery Medal

GREAT ACHIEVEMENT
A · W · A · R · D · S

Mitchell Lane
PUBLISHERS

P.O. Box 196
Hockessin, Delaware 19707

GREAT ACHIEVEMENT
A·W·A·R·D·S

Titles in the Series

Visit us on the web at www.mitchelllane.com
Comments? Email us at mitchelllane@mitchelllane.com

JOHN NEWBERY

and the Story of the Newbery Medal

GREAT ACHIEVEMENT
A·W·A·R·D·S

Printing   4   5   6   7   8   9

Library of Congress Cataloging-in-Publication Data

Roberts, Russell, 1953-
    John Newbery and the story of the Newbery Medal / Russell Roberts.
        p. cm. — (Great achievement awards)
    Summary: Profiles eighteenth-century British children's book publisher John Newbery and lists the winners of the award created in his honor from its inception in 1922 through 2003.
    Includes bibliographical references and index.
    ISBN 1-58415-201-X (library Bound)
        1. Newbery, John, 1713-1767. 2. Newbery Medal. 3. Children's literature—Publishing—England—History—18th century. 4. Children—Books and reading—Great Britain—History—18th century. [1. Newbery, John, 1713-1767. 2. Publishers and publishing. 3. Newbery medal books.] I. Title. II. Series.
    Z325.N53R63 2003
    028.5'079—dc21   2003004653

ABOUT THE AUTHOR: Russell Roberts has written and published books on a variety of subjects, including *Ten Days to a Sharper Memory, Discover the Hidden New Jersey*, and *Stolen! A History of Base Stealing*. He has also written several books for Mitchell Lane including *Pedro Menendez de Aviles* and *Bernardo de Galvez*. He lives in Bordentown, New Jersey with his family and a remarkably lazy, yet fiesty calico cat named Rusti.

PHOTO CREDITS: Cover: American Library association; p. 6 Corbis; p. 8 (left and right) Hulton/Archive; pp. 10, 12 Hulton/Archive; p. 14 Corbis; p. 18 Hulton/Archive; p. 21 Stephanie Kondrchek; pp. 22, 25, 26, 28, 32, 36 Hulton/Archive; p. 42 American Library Association.

PUBLISHER'S NOTE: The following story has been thoroughly researched and to the best of our knowledge represents a true story. Documentation of such research can be found on page 47.

To our knowledge, no images of John Newbery have survived through time. Should anyone know of the whereabouts of any such likeness, please contact the publisher.

The Web sites referenced in this book were all active as of the publication date. Because of the fleeting nature of some internet sites, we cannot guarantee they will be active when you are reading this book.

TABLE OF CONTENTS

When John Newbery decided to publish his first children's book in 1744, many other important things were happening in the world. A 15-year-old princess named Sophie Auguste Frederika von Anhalt-Zebst arrived in Russia. She would grow up to be Catherine the Great, one of the most important rulers in Russian history.

JOHN NEWBERY'S WONDERFUL IDEA

The year was 1744, and John Newbery, a bookseller and merchant in London, England, had a wonderful idea. It was an idea that is still affecting people today—especially kids. In fact, it is affecting you because you are reading this book.

Many other things happened in 1744. A 15-year-old princess named Sophie Auguste Frederika von Anhalt-Zebst arrived in Russia from her home in Stettin, Prussia (which is now a part of Poland) to get married to Grand Duke Peter of Holstein. This young girl would grow up to become Catherine the Great, one of the most important rulers in Russian history.

The year 1744 was also when Britain and France began fighting King George's War in North America to see which country would control the continent. It was the third war between the two countries in fifty-four years over this issue. Like the previous two, this war would not settle anything. It lasted for four years and when it ended conditions were about the same as when it had started. The struggle over control of North America finally ended when Britain defeated France in the French and Indian War (1754-1763).

In June, 1744, a British sea captain named George Anson returned home after sailing around the world. He began the voyage in September, 1740, with six ships. Only one of them completed the entire journey, but its hold was filled with treasure he'd captured from Spanish ships.

All these things were very important. So was John Newbery's idea. He decided to publish a book that would be fun for children to read.

This was a very risky decision for Newbery to make. What if no one liked the book? Then nobody would buy it and Newbery would lose money. If he lost too much money, he could be forced to stop printing books. He might even lose his business!

But Newbery was certain that children would like his book. The reason he felt this way was that it was a new kind of book. Before this, hardly anyone had ever written a book for kids to read and enjoy. It was thought that children's books should always teach something to the child. So books for kids were usually full of lessons.

Another type of children's books contained stories from years ago. These were ancient folktales or love stories that people used to pass down by word of mouth. They had originally been intended for adults. However, these stories were considered just tall tales invented by poor peasants, not serious literature for adults. They had been given to kids by default. But these stories had not been written with a child in mind.

There were also several novels, or works of fiction, that had been written for adults. Now they were thought of as children's books. *Robinson Crusoe* by Daniel Defoe and *Gulliver's Travels* by Jonathan Swift were examples of these. Their length and language made them unsuitable for youngsters who were just beginning to read.

Daniel Defoe (left) and Jonathan Swift (right) wrote books for adults, though today, their works are read by many children.

That's why a book that was strictly for the enjoyment and entertainment of children was something new.

Certainly, Newbery thought as he walked along the crowded London streets, the book should contain some lessons, such as about how good children get rewarded and bad children do not. But he would also make it fun for children to read. The book would also be attractive. It would have pretty pages with gold edges and flowers on them.

So Newbery kept thinking as he walked. Lost in thought, he did not notice the herd of sheep being driven noisily down the street. He did not notice the merchants crying out what they were selling from their pushcarts, or the children playing in the street, or even the people sleeping on the sidewalk. He didn't even hear the roaring of lions in the great Tower of London. Its shadow fell onto him, but it did not darken his sunny enthusiasm. The more Newbery thought about his idea, the more he liked it: a fun book for children. It could work! It should work!

And it did work. Before long, he was publishing many books that were intended just for children. They sold very well. Newbery never had to worry about people ignoring them. Soon he became well-known as a children's book publisher.

In fact, John Newbery became so famous from publishing children's books that a medal was named after him: the Newbery Medal. It is awarded to the best children's book written each year. Children around the world, and especially those who love to read, have him to thank whenever they enjoy a book that is written especially for them.

One of London's most famous landmarks, St. Paul's Cathedral on the River Thames was designed by British architect Sir Christopher Wren. The building was completed in 1710. This drawing is of the most recent cathedral to occupy this site since the 7th century. The others were destroyed by fire. The large dome is modeled after the Pantheon in Rome. Both Wren and the famous British naval hero Admiral Horatio Nelson are buried in the cathedral.

A FARMER'S SON

E ven though John Newbery was the son of an English farmer, it is not surprising that he became a famous book publisher. One of his ancestors was Ralph (or Rafe) Newberie. He was one of the most respected book publishers in England in the latter half of the sixteenth century. No wonder that John Newbery had printer's ink running through his veins!

John Newbery was born on July 9, 1713, in the village of Waltham St. Lawrence, a small village located several miles west of London. His father was Robert Newbery, a farmer. Unfortunately his mother's first name is unknown.

The village of Waltham St. Lawrence is still a quiet, peaceful place today. Three country lanes meet there, as if urging travelers to stay a while and visit the tiny town. It is still the type of place where a boy like John Newbery can run through green fields and dream about exciting adventures in faraway places. But most people pass quickly through Waltham St. Lawrence without stopping there.

Not very much is known about Newbery's boyhood. As a farmer's son, it is likely that his education was very basic. The sons of village farmers were usually expected to become farmers when they grew up, just like their fathers.

But Newbery was different. He did not want to become a farmer. He wanted instead to become a merchant, someone who sold things to people. Years later, John Newbery's son Francis said that his father was interested

This painting is of the Old London Bridge, circa 1705. This was the first bridge across the Thames River, which divides London. Begun in 1176, it took 33 years to build, finally being completed in 1209. The bridge was built of stone, was 926 feet wide, had 19 stone arches, and was the longest inhabited bridge in Europe, containing stores and houses. By 1358 it had over 135 shops and houses on it, and was home to thousands of people. The famous playwright William Shakespeare lived on London Bridge for a time. But London Bridge began falling down when large pieces of ice hit it and destroyed some parts, along with some of the shops and houses. Fire also destroyed parts of it. Although it was repaired, eventually erosion over time made it unsafe. In 1832, it was ordered that a new bridge be built.

in too many other things as a boy to become a farmer. He was good at math and knew how to spell and write. He probably enjoyed reading too.

At the age of sixteen Newbery left home to find his way in the world. He walked ten miles further west to the town of Reading (which is pronounced RED-ing). There he got a job as an assistant to William Ayres, who was the publisher of a newspaper called the *Reading Mercury*. It was Newbery's first job in publishing.

Reading was nothing like Waltham St. Lawrence. The town sat at the intersection of the Thames and Kennet rivers, and that location made it very busy. Many people came to Reading to buy and sell crops, animals, and other things. At that time, the town was reported to have one of the best markets in all of England for finding grain. It was also known for manufacturing cloth and malt, an ingredient used in making liquor. In future years, Reading would become a booming, bustling manufacturing town.

At the time that Newbery got a job there in 1730, the *Mercury* was a very respected local newspaper. It had been founded just seven years earlier by two printers, W. Parks and D. Kinnier.

Parks went to the American colonies the year after he helped to establish the newspaper, but Kinnier continued to publish the paper. At some point William Ayres took over from Kinnier. Ayres obviously liked what he saw in the young man fresh off the farm, and gave him a job.

So even though he was only 16 years old, Newbery already found himself involved in publishing. It would not take very long for him to become involved in many other things as well.

This ad for Hamlin Wizard Oil is an example of the patent medicines sold in the 18th century. Patent medicines were products that were sold without a doctor's prescription. They often claimed to cure a broad variety of illnesses. Patent medicines were popular in the days before the wide availability of doctors, and before medical science was very advanced. Once the federal government passed laws in the early 20th century that said manufacturers of medicines could not make false claims about their products and had to list the ingredients, the patent medicine industry collapsed.

NEWBERY THE MERCHANT

A lthough it is known that William Ayres was the publisher of the *Mercury* who gave Newbery his first job, it is a mystery when Ayres turned over the newspaper to William Carnan. However, by February of 1737 Carnan was publishing the *Mercury*.

By then Newbery had been working at the newspaper for nearly seven years. During this time, he became a valuable employee, as well as a trusted friend of Carnan. When Carnan died at the end of 1737, he left his personal estate to two people: his brother Charles and Newbery.

Carnan's death left his wife, Mary, and their three children— Thomas, John, and Anna-Maria—without a man to care for them. But Mary Carnan and Newbery became attracted to each other, and before long they were married.

It was quite common at this time in England for an assistant to marry the widow of his boss. Both sides benefited: The assistant inherited the business so that it would continue running and the wife had a man to provide for her and her children. This was at a time when women did not work.

Newbery and Mary would eventually have three children of their own: Mary, born in March 1740, John, born in September 1741, and Francis, born on July 6, 1743. Unfortunately, John fell down some stone steps when he was a boy and badly hurt his spine. He died when he was just 11 years old.

John Newbery seems to have been a kind father. He treated his children very easily when the philosophy of the day was "spare the rod and spoil the child." He supported his youngest son Francis for five years while the boy went to school at Oxford and Cambridge. These were two very famous and expensive colleges even back then. A man who attended them was almost certain of a fine career when he graduated.

Francis Newbery, however, did not graduate with a degree from either school. Yet John Newbery does not seem to have been upset with his son for spending so much time at the schools and not graduating. In fact, he left his publishing business to him in his will.

After he took over the *Mercury* newspaper, Newbery became a very busy man. His boyhood dreams of becoming a merchant had come true. He sold many different goods and services from his Reading location at the Bible and Crown in the Market Place and used the *Mercury* to advertise them.

One of the businesses that Newbery operated was a printing business. In 1741, the *Mercury* contained an advertisement for the printing services of Newbery and his partner, C. Micklewright. The ad said that they performed printing "in the Neatest Manner."

Printing was just a part of Newbery's many different businesses. In September 1740, the *Mercury* contained the following ad which gives an example of another one: "John Newbery at the *Bible and Crown* in the Market Place, Reading, keeps a wholesale warehouse, and furnishes shopkeepers with all sorts of haberdashery goods (these included small items such as threads, tapes, bindings, ribbons, pins, needles) as cheap as in London. And any person by sending a letter to him will be as well served as if they came in person."

Another advertisement in the newspaper in 1741 was for a newly invented "blacking ball for shoes." This early version of a shoeshine kit was supposed to give shoes a "fine Gloss (shine), black as jet." It was also supposed to help protect the shoe against wet weather and make it last longer.

Newbery had also established a bustling business selling patent medicines. These are medicines that are not prescribed by a doctor. They often had strange names and claimed to work on many illnesses. One of these was called *Daffy's Elixir Salutis*. It was supposed to be good for numerous ailments, including coughs, colds, indigestion, and "fits of the Mother," a commonly used term at that time for hysteria.

Of course, Newbery did not forget his first love: book publishing. In 1740, with his partner Micklewright, he published a book called *The Whole Duty of Man, Laid Down in a Plain and Familiar Way, for the Use of All, but Especially the Meanest Reader*. This was a reprint of a book published several decades earlier by an English clergyman named Richard Allestree. It was a guide to having good manners.

On a lighter note, in that same year Newbery also published a book entitled *Miscellaneous Works for the Amusement of the Fair Sex*. At that time the phrase "fair sex" referred to women. While it is unclear what this book was about, the title indicates that it was a collection of stories, poems, and other types of writing that women would enjoy reading.

All of these things—book publishing, printing, producing the *Mercury* newspaper, selling numerous types of goods, and raising a family with several children—kept Newbery very busy. It seemed that his life was full.

But John Newbery was not a person to stand still and let things just happen. Even as he was so involved with everything, he was planning for the greatest adventure of his life: moving to England's capital city of London.

The Tower of London, circa 1740, shown with River Thames in the foreground. The Tower of London was begun in 1078 by William the Conqueror. He wanted to build a castle inside a fort so that future kings could live safely. After his death, other kings built other towers and castles around the castle that William had built, and all together the buildings became known as the Tower of London. In John Newbery's time there was a tower called the Lion Tower, where animals like lions, elephants, and bears were kept. The Tower of London was also used as a prison for a time, and executions were held there. Today, it is a tourist attraction where the priceless Crown Jewels are kept.

NEWBERY'S TRIP

Before moving to London, however, Newbery went on a month-long trip that seems to have had several purposes. One was to advertise, or spread the word, about his businesses in Reading, so as to increase his customers. The second reason he went on the trip was to gave him ideas and feed his active imagination. Newbery was extremely curious, and it seems as if the trip was partly to sightsee, like a tourist, and partly to discover additional goods and services that he thought he could sell.

He set off on his journey on July 9, 1740. Fortunately, he wrote down many things about this trip in a small volume he called his "Private Memorandum Book." So today there is a specific account of what he did on the trip. It is one of the few times in Newbery's life that exact details of his life are available.

His trip took him first to London, and then to numerous other towns in England. Along the way he very carefully noted such things as the distance between towns and made personal observations about the journey. For example, when he traveled from the town of Grantham to Lincoln, he wrote "you cross a delicious plain, in length about 22 miles...in the whole 22 miles there is but one village (called Ancaster)." He also wrote that the long trip made him very thirsty. When he asked a man traveling with him if he could share some of his drink, the person "would not spare one spoonful."

He also saw some unusual things. Mechanical engines were very rare at the time, and Newbery apparently passed a building that contained two fiery, smoking engines. The sight of the noisy mechanical marvels thrilled him. In one town he saw a "dunking stool" that seems to have been used to punish women who yelled at their husbands. If they hollered and complained too much, the women were tied to the stool and dunked under water! This shows how poorly women were often treated at this time.

Everywhere in his Private Memorandum Book Newbery jotted down notes about things he wanted to sell and upcoming plans to publish various pieces of literature. He was an extremely energetic person, and the jottings in his notebook show his busy, active mind at work. He was bursting with a hundred ideas, and the thoughts flowed from his pen like water from a fountain.

He wrote notes to advertise goods (haberdashery and cutlery such as knives and forks) for sale at cheap, wholesale prices upon his return home. He wrote about plans to publish two new newspapers, as well as books about the history of the world and famous sayings from the languages of other cultures. He recorded recipes for medicines, some for personal use and some for possible sale. He also made notes about books he himself wanted to read, both for entertainment and education.

Newbery's Private Memorandum Book gives modern-day historians an understanding of why he was able to successfully publish books for children. It shows him to be a person who was always ready to consider new ideas and then take chances on them. Children's literature was certainly a new and unproven idea at this time. It took somebody like Newbery, unafraid of taking risks, to try it.

When Newbery returned to Reading in the middle of August, he carried out many of the ideas and schemes that he had thought up during his trip. Still in partnership with C. Micklewright, he published several new books. He started another newspaper called the *Reading Journal and Weekly Review,* although it did not last long. He also signed an agreement with a man named John Hooper so he could begin selling "female pills" with his medicines.

Newbery's various schemes kept him busy in Reading for several more years. Then in the year 1744 there is an advertisement that he has opened a warehouse at the following address: Bible and Crown, near Devereux Court, without Temple Bar. The place? London.

He had made his big move.

This map shows many of the places that Newbery traveled to or lived in during his lifetime.

London during the 1750s was perhaps the greatest city in the world. The population was growing fast. By 1801, more than one million people lived in and around London. Three decades later, the population had grown by another million.

LONDON IN NEWBERY'S TIME

L ondon was as different from the peaceful little village of Newbery's birthplace of Waltham St. Lawrence as a tiny kitten is from a roaring lion. It was the largest city in Europe. It has been estimated that its population in 1750, just six years after Newbery moved there, was about 650,000. More people lived in just one or two London blocks than in all of Waltham St. Lawrence. It was a busy, bustling, noisy city, and for an ambitious merchant like John Newbery, it was the best possible place to be.

One of the most interesting things about London was its streets. There was a law that required every citizen of London to pave a portion of the street up to the center of the front of his house. Not everyone obeyed this law, and even if they did, the results were often very different. The cobblestones usually used for paving might be smooth and even in front of one house, and bumpy and full of holes in front of another. The result was a crazy-quilt combination of cobblestones and no cobblestones, a roller coaster of up and down stones. People walking on the street often were stepping in holes or even mud. The effect was like walking on an uneven funhouse floor that rises up and suddenly dips down.

People often threw whatever they wanted into the streets, from trash and small dead animals to pots filled with human waste! On top of this, the streets were often filled with piles of animal manure. This came from the horses people used to ride and pull wagons and carriages as well as from herds of livestock such as cattle, pigs and sheep that farmers would drive through the city on their way to market.

It's not surprising that the streets of London were often a mess. In 1742, the famous American inventor and statesman Benjamin Franklin was in London. He found that when the streets were wet and it was hard to see what was lying in them, "there was no crossing [the street] but in paths kept clean by poor people with brooms," according to Liza Picard's book *Dr. Johnson's London.*

Many of the stores and shops of London identified themselves with a heavy wooden sign mounted to an iron pole that stuck straight out from the building. When the wind blew, the sign would swing back and forth. Unfortunately, the signs often broke off their poles, and came crashing down to the sidewalk. If the signs hit somebody standing below them, the person could be seriously injured.

Unfortunately, there often **was** somebody standing below. The streets and sidewalks of London were packed with people. There were merchants selling their goods out of push-carts, housewives and servants rushing to stores and back home, children playing, livestock herders running back and forth to keep their animals from going astray, the poor and ill hunched or lying down in doorways, and horse-drawn carriages carrying people and supplies. They all fought for a tiny bit of space on the narrow streets and sidewalks.

Adding to this mass of traffic was that many people who could afford to do so used what were called "sedan chairs" to go from place to place. These were enclosed chairs with two sets of poles supporting them that people entered in the comfort of their own homes. Husky men called bearers would then carry these people to their destination, like carriages without horses. People used this method of transportation so that they would not have to walk on the streets or sidewalks.

With all of this animal and human traffic, London was an incredibly noisy place. Many of the wagons clattering up and down the street had iron tires. These made a loud noise when they struck the cobblestones, and added to the sounds of people talking, merchants crying out the prices of their wares, children shouting, and animals snorting, mooing and squealing.

Of course, in such crowded conditions as these it was easy to get robbed by quick-handed thieves. Everyone who went outdoors had to be very aware of pickpockets who could dip a hand into a pocket or handbag and steal a wallet in the blink of an eye. Often the pickpocket was a child.

Criminals were especially bold because there was no police force to watch out for them. The streets were patrolled only at night and then just by a group of elderly men called the Watch. They carried lanterns, and their chief duty was to call out the time.

The most impressive thing about London was its size. Buildings were everywhere, from the great royal residences such as St. James Palace to old, dilapidated buildings that sometimes fell down on people's heads when they tried to live in them.

The palace sat across from St. James Park. Even though this was a royal park, the king allowed people to use it. However, they had to walk, and not use carriages, horses or chairs.

Even though he came from a small city himself, nothing could have prepared John Newbery for the sights and sounds of London. It was the biggest, loudest, and busiest city in the world, and its constant hustle-and-bustle was both exciting and terrifying.

But Newbery did not care. He was in the best possible place for a merchant to be located. There were customers and opportunities every-where. Now he could really begin to put his plans of business success into operation.

One of these plans was to lead to the establishment of children's literature.

This illustration depicts pickpockets diving in a street near St. James Palace, London.

A LITTLE PRETTY
POCKET-BOOK,

INTENDED FOR THE
INSTRUCTION and AMUSEMENT

OF

LITTLE MASTER TOMMY,

AND

PRETTY MISS POLLY.

With Two LETTERS from
JACK the GIANT-KILLER;

AS ALSO

A BALL and PINCUSHION;

The Use of which will infallibly make TOMMY
a good Boy, and POLLY a good Girl.

To which is added,

A LITTLE SONG-BOOK,

BEING

A NEW ATTEMPT to teach CHILDREN
the Use of the English Alphabet, by Way
of Diversion.

THE FIRST *WORCESTER* EDITION.

PRINTED at WORCESTER, *Maſſachuſetts.*
By ISAIAH THOMAS,
And SOLD, Wholeſale and Retail, at his Book-
Store. MDCCLXXXVII.

This is the cover of John Newbery's first book for children, A Little Pretty
Pocket-Book. *This particular cover is from an edition published in America
at Worcester, Massachusetts.*

CHAPTER 6

A LITTLE PRETTY POCKET BOOK

Newbery did not remain long at the Bible and Crown, his first London address. He had also opened a second location at the Golden Ball, in Castle Alley at the Royal Exchange, but he left that one as well. No one knows why he moved. Possibly these addresses were too far away from the center of London's business community.

His last advertisement at his old address was on July 24, 1745. A few weeks later, a newspaper advertisement listed his new address as "The Bible and Sun, near the Chapter House, in St. Paul's Church-yard." St. Paul's Churchyard was an important business and publishing center in London. This is the address that would become famous in the world of children's literature. Later, when the London authorities put numbers on the buildings, this address became #65.

By this time, Newbery's many business affairs were overwhelming even him. Though he was now living in London, he was still trying to also run his businesses at Reading. But the pressures of running two such widely separated locations in an age long before telephones and e-mail proved impossible. He sold the Reading businesses, and concentrated solely on his London operations.

It was still too much. Newbery had to reduce his business efforts still further. He decided to sell just two types of products: patent medicines and books.

His patent medicine business was very successful. He sold over two dozen medicines. His best seller was called *Dr. James's Fever Powder.*

This was a very popular product that people took to cure a fever. Newbery was the only person who sold it.

Some people believed greatly in this powder. According to Charles Welsh's *book A Bookseller of the Last Century,* British writer Horace Walpole said, "I have such faith in these powders that I believe I should take them if the house were on fire." Another person who liked the powder was the poet Christopher Smart. He dedicated his poem *Hymn to the Supreme Being* to Dr. James because he thought that the fever powder had helped him recover from a serious illness.

Robert James, the fever powder's inventor, was a well-known doctor. He became friendly with Newbery because he wrote books and Newbery was a publisher. In fact, the two became such good friends that Newbery did a big favor for Dr. James. At one time, the doctor had sold a share of his fever powder business to someone else to raise money. Newbery repurchased that share and gave it to Dr. James.

The success of his patent medicine business brought him a strange kind of fame. Some people, including his family back in Waltham St. Lawrence, considered him an expert on the subjects of health and sickness—even for animals!

Christopher Smart was born in 1722. As a young man, he lectured at the prestigious Cambridge University. He moved to London where he worked as a poet, editor, and writer. Unfortunately, he suffered a mental breakdown, and was in and out of asylums for several years. Eventually, he was put in prison because he owed money. He died there in 1771.

In the year 1752, the horses and cattle in Waltham St. Lawrence began getting sick. Many people, including his brother Robert, wrote letters to Newbery asking him how to cure them. What Newbery said or did in response is unknown. But he did take a trip back to his boyhood town either late in 1752 or early in 1753. Whether or not he helped cure the animals is a mystery.

Selling patent medicines was only half of Newbery's business. The other half was book publishing.

And he was about to make book publishing history.

His first book for children was called *A Little Pretty Pocket-Book*. It was published in 1744. Many people consider this as the date when children's literature began.

Since so little is known about Newbery's life, it is uncertain why he decided to publish *A Little Pretty Pocket-Book.* Based on the history of events that were occurring at about that time, scholars think they understand the "why" behind Newbery's decision.

Newbery was not the first one to publish children's books. In 1694 someone named "J.G." published a book called *A Playbook for Children*. A few years later, in 1702, a person known only by the initials "T.W." published *A Little Book for Little Children.* A third person who published books for kids was Thomas Boreman. Between 1740 and 1743 he came out with a series of books called *Gigantick Histories.*

But these books were all single attempts. It is unclear how successful these other books were. After they were published, there was no plan to keep producing children's books.

Newbery was the first person to successfully publish books for kids—and even more important, to keep publishing them on a somewhat regular basis. He was the first to make people realize that children could be just as important an audience as adults when it came to selling books.

Several factors helped Newbery succeed where others had failed. One was that people began having a different feeling about children at this time. People realized that young kids were like a blank piece of paper. They had few thoughts or ideas of their own, and were waiting to be "written on" by the actions or words of others. Parents began to understand that they could influence their children's development by how they treated them. One way to do this was to give them books that contained a moral message.

Another factor that helped Newbery was that the "middle class" was developing in England at this time. More and more people were making enough money to live comfortable lives. While they weren't rich, they weren't poor either. They were in the middle.

They wanted their children to grow up to get even better jobs than they did. They thought that Newbery's books, with their messages of hard work and good conduct, would help their kids grow up to be more successful. Newbery realized this. His books always contained a lesson of some kind. Some of these lessons were that good children get rewarded, bad children get punished, and hard work is its own reward.

But even while his books contained lessons, they also were fun for children to read. The front page of *A Little Pretty Pocket-Book* said that it was intended for the "instruction and amusement of Little Master Tommy (boys) and Pretty Miss Polly (girls)," and that's exactly how Newbery wanted it. The book was supposed to be both educational **and** fun.

To reinforce his point, Newbery put a saying in Latin on the first page: *Delectando monemus.* That means "instruction with delight."

Newbery explained his feelings in the opening pages of *A Little Pretty Pocket-Book.* He wrote that children should be raised in the following way: "The grand design in the nurture (bringing up) of children is to make them *strong, hardy, healthy, virtuous, wise and happy;* and these good purposes are not to be obtained without some care and management in their infancy."

A Little Pretty Pocket-Book contained a series of rhymes in alphabetical order based on children's games. This was the rhyme about the letter "B":

Base-Ball

The *Ball* once struck off,

Away flies (runs) the *Boy*

To the next destin'd Post,

And then Home with Joy.

Below each rhyme for each letter was a moral, or lesson, also in rhyme. The moral for the baseball rhyme was that even if people leave home on a journey, they will come back if they have good memories.

Each page had an illustration. The illustration for the "B" rhyme showed three boys playing a game that is most likely base-ball.

These illustrations were woodcuts. This means that the picture was carved into a piece of wood. The wood was then inked and stamped on paper. This was an expensive process. It was the only method of printing identical pieces of artwork at that time.

Another reason that kids liked the book was that it looked pretty. It was smaller than most books. Newbery called it a "pocket-book," because it could fit in a pocket. That way, kids felt it was made just for them.

In addition, Newbery used expensive, gold-edged paper from Holland to print the book. The book's title, *A Little Pretty Pocket-Book,* described it perfectly.

Newbery even included a toy with the book, at an additional cost. He offered a ball for boys and a pincushion for girls.

Although it is unknown how many copies of *A Little Pretty Pocket-Book* were sold, it was very popular. Newbery had shown that children's literature was every bit as important as books for adults. It is a lesson that book publishers are still listening to today.

Dr. Samuel Johnson with his Scottish biographer James Boswell and the Irish playwright Oliver Goldsmith at the Mitre Tavern, shown in an illustration by Eyre Crowe, 1770. These three men were members of The Club, a literary organization founded by Samuel Johnson in 1764. Boswell became a great friend and admirer of Johnson, and in 1791 he published a book called the Life of Samuel Johnson, *one of the greatest biographies ever written.*

A Very Busy Man

Wﾐith the success of *A Pretty Little Pocket-Book,* Newbery became even busier than before. According to Welsh's book, Newbery's son Francis wrote that his father was "in the full employment (use) of his talents in writing and publishing books of amusement and instruction for children. The call for them was immense, an edition of many thousands being sometimes exhausted (sold out) during the Christmas holidays."

Because he was a book publisher, Newbery was friendly with many writers of the period. One of these was the poet Christopher Smart. The two men were the authors of a magazine called *The Midwife, or the Old Woman's Magazine.* Later, Newbery helped Smart when the poet became ill.

Another writer who was Newbery's friend was Samuel Johnson, one of the greatest literary figures in English history. In 1755 Johnson published his epic book *Dictionary of the English Language.* Johnson occasionally borrowed money from Newbery, and he once "repaid" his friend by poking some fun at him.

Johnson wrote a series of essays called *The Idler* for a newspaper called the *Universal Chronicle, or Weekly Gazette.* Newbery had started it and remained part owner.

Essay #19 of *The Idler* was a humorous story about a man called Jack Whirler who was constantly rushing from place to place. Later, Newbery's son Francis said that the character of Jack Whirler was based on his father. Although Johnson exaggerated the activities of Jack Whirler to make him even funnier, the essay provides a glimpse of how busy Newbery was during this time.

Johnson writes that Jack Whirler is a person "whose business keeps him in perpetual motion." He says that Jack Whirler "cannot stand still because he is wanted in another place, and who is wanted in many places because he stays in none." Because Whirler has more businesses than he can operate from one house, he has two houses. However, he is so busy that he is never at **either** house.

In one of the essay's most humorous passages, Johnson writes that when Jack Whirler visits his friends, it is only to tell them that he will come back tomorrow. But when he returns the next day, he tells them that he cannot stay. "So short are his visits that he seldom appears to have come for any other reason but to say he must go," writes Johnson.

According to Johnson, Jack Whirler never eats a full meal at one sitting. He no sooner sits down and takes a bite then he has to rush somewhere else, where he takes another bite.

Johnson also says that even though Jack Whirler is overwhelmed with business, he wants more. Every time that he thinks of a new idea, it takes total control of him. He puts all of his thought and energy into it until it is almost finished. Then, when the idea is just about perfected, it is dropped in favor of a new idea. The cycle begins again.

"Thus Jack Whirler lives in perpetual fatigue," concludes Johnson.

It was certainly not Johnson's intention to criticize Newbery. Johnson liked him too much to do that. It was just that Newbery's life was extremely hectic and active, or Johnson would not have thought about writing the essay in the first place.

Many people who have such hectic lives become stressed and irritable. Not John Newbery. Most written accounts agree that Newbery was a very pleasant man. We can imagine him not being angry, but laughing, over the Jack Whirler essay, especially if his life was anything close to what Johnson described. According to Francis Newbery, his reaction to being portrayed as Jack Whirler was to good-naturedly threaten to get even with Johnson. He said he would publish an essay of his own about Johnson. But Newbery never did. He was probably too busy!

"Jack Whirler" describes Newbury's life. But what about the man himself? What type of a person was John Newbery?

Unfortunately, there are very few clues about Newbery the man. Like much else about his life, his personality and behavior are basically unknown.

However, there are a few bits of information about him. His son Francis writes that he was a polite, good-humored man with a very generous nature. He was very kind to people less fortunate than himself. Newbery always carried a book and pen, which he probably used to write down the many ideas and inspirations that came to him.

Others say that he was always loaning money to writers who needed it. He was very honest in his dealings with people, and was sometimes known as "Honest John Newbery." Welsh writes that still others have called him a "man of genius."

Oliver Goldsmith was a poet, playwright, and novelist born in 1730 in Ireland. He taught school and practiced medicine before becoming a fulltime writer. He eventually became one of the original members of the literary group called The Club, founded by Samuel Johnson. He died in 1774.

NEWBERY'S FINAL YEARS

I n the period that began in 1750 and lasted until his death in 1767, Newbery published most of his children's books. About two dozen books appeared during these years, with names like *Nurse Truelove's Christmas Box, The Renowned History of Giles Gingerbread,* and his most famous title, *The Renowned History of Little Goody Two-Shoes.* Newbery published so many books for children that he truly was "their old friend in St. Paul's Churchyard," as John Rowe Townsend in *John Newbery and His Books* says he once described himself.

His patent medicine business was also continuing to do very well during this period. Newbery often used his books, even the ones for children, as commercials for his medicines. Sometimes the mention of his medicines in the books was not strictly an advertisement, but woven into the book's story as an actual part of the plot.

For example, when Goody Two-Shoes's father died of a bad fever, it was because Newbery's well-known medicine Dr. James's Fever Powder was not available. The message, of course, was that if the powder had been able to be used, the father would have been cured.

In 1751, Newbery, who had started a new branch of literature with his children's books, started something else new for kids when he published the first children's magazine. It was called *The Lilliputian Magazine.* It contained stories, fairy tales, songs, riddles and jokes. Unfortunately, the magazine only lasted for a few issues, but another entirely new industry had emerged from the active mind of John Newbery.

Even as he was involved with other projects, Newbery continued to publish children's books. He produced them at an uneven rate. One year he might publish three new books, and another year two. Some years there were none.

One great mystery about the Newbery books is trying to figure out who actually wrote them. In Newbery's time, it was very common for book authors not to identify themselves. Newbery's children's books were like this; the author names are obviously made-up.

For example, the book titled *FOOD for the Mind: Or, A NEW RIDDLE BOOK* was supposedly written by "John THE GIANT-KILLER." Other names used were "Tom Telescope," "Giles Gingerbread" and "Woglog the Great Giant." This has made it very difficult for scholars to identify who actually wrote the books.

There are several theories about the actual writer. Some say that it is Oliver Goldsmith, a well-known English writer of the time, who met Newbery in 1757 or 1758. Goldsmith wrote many books in which he did not use his own name. Because he did other writing work for Newbery, many experts believe that he wrote most, if not all, of the children's books. In addition, Goldsmith, like Samuel Johnson, sometimes borrowed money from Newbery. Since the two men knew each other so well, it is possible that Goldsmith is the author.

Others say that the brothers Giles and Griffith Jones wrote the Newbery books. Like Goldsmith, they were writers who also wrote books for other people. An article from that period claimed that the Joneses were responsible for the children's books. In addition, in 1794 Stephen Jones, the son of Giles Jones, claimed that his father and uncle wrote *Goody Two-Shoes*.

Another group of people feel that the author of the Newbery children's books is Newbery himself! There is some evidence to support this theory. Goldsmith once wrote about a bookseller who had written many little books for children. Since Goldsmith knew Newbery so well, people feel that he was talking about his friend.

Another reason for thinking that Newbery himself might be the author is that all of his books have what people consider "a personality." They are all friendly, happy books with a lot of humor, just as people describe Newbery himself.

There may be another clue. In June 1762, he went with his son Francis on a trip to Oxford University. While he was there, Newbery had dinner with two of his son's friends and a professor of poetry. During the evening, the professor took out a strange-looking, pointy striped cap and placed it on his head. He looked so silly that everyone laughed, and asked him where he gotten the funny cap.

The professor explained that he was a member of "The Jelly Bag Society." This was a special club at the college. All members of the club wore the cap. The professor further explained that the unusual name came from a poem that had been written and published by John Newbery. So the professor was wearing the cap in honor of Newbery.

Upon hearing this Newbery got embarrassed and blushed. No name had been given as the writer of the poem. But Newbery said that while he did not know how they had discovered it, he had written the poem.

If he wrote poems such as this one, his supporters say, he could also have written the ones that appeared in his children's books.

The biggest reason against Newbery writing the books is simply that he was so busy. When would he have found the time?

Unfortunately, it will probably never be known who actually wrote the books. The truth will most likely remain a literary mystery, just as it has been for over 250 years.

Still eager for new business, in 1764 Newbery took out a patent (which keeps someone from copying an invention) on a machine for "printing, staining and colouring silk stuffs, linens, cottons, leather and paper" along with two other men. Some experts on Newbery's life say that the description of this machine makes it sound like an early version of a color printing press. At that time, all printing presses were black and white. Color printing would not become possible for many years. However, it is unknown what became of this machine.

In 1765 and 1766 Newbery published some of his most famous children's books, including *The Renowned History of GILES GINGER-BREAD* and *The Renowned History of Little GOODY TWO-SHOES*.

The following year, 1767, Newbery published several more children's books. But these books would be his last. Although there are no details about the circumstances of his death, Newbery was worried enough about his health that in October of 1767 he made his will in case he should die. He made further changes to it in November. Newbery was very concerned that his businesses would be in good hands in the event of his death. By now he was in the care of Dr. James.

But despite the doctor's efforts, Newbery's health got worse. His son Francis was called home from school at Oxford to be with his father. Newbery continued to get sicker, until he died at the age of 54 on December 22, 1767. He was buried in the churchyard of his childhood home in Waltham St. Lawrence.

Francis wrote that people were upset and saddened by his father's death. Many of the newspapers of the time expressed regret at his death, noting that he had died at the young age of 54.

When Newbery died, his will directed that his businesses go to his son, a nephew, and his stepson. Unfortunately, these three men were not friends.

Newbery left his patent medicine business to his son Francis. In his will, he also asked that his son Francis, stepson Thomas Carnan, and nephew Francis continue publishing and selling books. But the three men obviously did not get along, because soon after Newbery's death, nephew Francis opened a book shop at 20 Ludgate Street in London and began publishing books on his own. Sons Francis and Thomas continued the store at St. Paul's Churchyard. That the brothers and the cousin did not get along soon became painfully obvious. When Carnan and Newbery published a book called *New History of England* in 1772, they included a page in the book that pointed out that they had nothing to do with Francis Newbery at Ludgate Street. They also included a second page that told people that their cousin Francis Newbery had no interest in John Newbery's books for children!

But literary historians also think that Newbery's sons Francis and Thomas did not get along, either. In particular, Thomas felt that John Newbery had not been fair to him in his will. Finally, around 1782, Thomas began publishing books all by himself.

Son Francis Newbery eventually operated only the patent medicine business. Nephew Francis Newbery continued publishing books on his own until he died in 1780. Sadly, even though John Newbery had built a business based on the smiles of delighted children, that business does not seem to have brought much delight to the family he left behind.

The Newbery Medal, named for the 18th century bookseller, John Newbery, is one of the most prestigious awards a children's book author can receive. It is awarded each year by the American Library Association to the author of the most distinguished children's book published the previous year. Honor books are also cited.

REMEMBERING JOHN NEWBERY

A lthough he was dead, John Newbery was not forgotten. The children's books he had printed took on a life of their own. They began a whole new industry of children's book publishing. Over the years, the industry continued to grow. More and more things were published for children: songbooks, fairy tales, nursery rhymes, animal stories, poetry—anything that publishers thought a child would like to read. And it was all because of Newbery.

Finally, in June of 1921, a publisher named Frederic C. Melcher decided that something should be done to honor John Newbery. He suggested that the Children's Library Section of the American Library Association should give an award to the author of the most distinguished children's book that had been published the previous year. The award would be called the John Newbery Medal.

The librarians all thought it was an excellent idea. The Executive Board of the American Library Association approved it the following year. The Board also agreed with Melcher's statement of the award's purpose, which appears on the ALA website: "To encourage original creative work in the field of books for children. To emphasize to the public that contributions to the literature for children deserve similar recognition to poetry, plays, or novels. To give those librarians, who make it their life work to serve children's reading interests, an opportunity to encourage good writing in this field."

The winner the first year was Hendrik Willem van Loon. He wrote a history book called *The Story of Mankind*.

The award has been given every year since then, which makes it the oldest award for children's books in the world. The winner receives a medal. On the front is an engraving that shows Newbery with Little Master Tommy and Pretty Miss Polly from *A Little Pretty Pocket-Book.* The winner's name and date are engraved on the reverse side.

The committee that decides on the award-winning book has a hard decision to make because there are so many good children's books published every year. In addition to the medal-winning book, up to six other books are also recognized. Up to 1971, these were called "runners-up." Ever since then, they have been known as "honor books."

Both the medal-winner and the honor books display a blue spot on their spines. In addition, a label on their front covers identifies the book as a medal or honor winner and also includes the year of its award.

The award keeps Newbery's name alive, so that people today still remember this eighteenth century English publisher and bookseller who specialized in children's books. More importantly, every time you get a book out of the library, or buy a book at the store, or read a book such as this one, you are demonstrating all over again that Newbery was right: children are important, and publishing books just for them is a good thing to do.

For understanding that, John Newbery was truly a man of genius.

THE NEWBERY MEDAL

The John Newbery Medal is awarded annually by the American Library Association to the book judged to be the most outstanding contribution to American children's literature during the past year. The book can be of any type—fiction, non-fiction, poetry, etc.—but it must be an original (not a reprint of an existing book or a translation of a book in another language, for example). In addition, the author must be a citizen or resident of the United States.

1922 – Hendrick Willem van Loon – *The Story of Mankind*

1923 – Hugh Lofting – *The Voyages of Doctor Dolittle*

1924 – Charles Boardman Hawes – *The Dark Frigate*

1925 – Charles J. Finger – *Tales from Silver Lands*

1926 – Arthur Bowie Chrisman – *Shen of the Sea*

1927 – Will James – *Smoky, the Cowhorse*

1928 – Dham Gopal Mukerji – *Gay-Neck, the Story of a Pigeon*

1929 – Eric P. Kelly – *The Trumpeter of Krakow*

1930 – Rachel Field – *Hitty, her First Hundred Years*

1931 – Elizabeth Coatsworth – *The Cat who Went to Heaven*

1932 – Laura Adams Armer – *Waterless Mountain*

1933 – Elizabeth Foreman Lewis – *Young Fu of the Upper Yangtse*

1934 – Cornelia Meigs – *Invincible Louisa*

1935 – Monica Shannon – *Dobry*

1936 – Carol Ryrie Brink – *Caddie Woodlawn*

1937 – Ruth Sawyer – *Roller Skates*

1938 – Kate Seredy – *The White Stag*

1939 – Elizabeth Enright – *Thimble Summer*

1940 – James Daugherty – *Daniel Boone*

1941 – Armstrong Sperry – *Call it Courage*

1942 – Walter D. Edmonds – *The Matchlock Gun*

1943 – Elizabeth Janet Gray – *Adam of the Road*

1944 – Esther Forbes – *Johnny Tremain*

1945 – Robert Lawson – *Rabbit Hill*

1946 – Lois Lenski – *Strawberry Girl*

1947 – Carolyn Sherwin Bailey – *Miss Hickory*

1948 – William Pène du Bois – *The Twenty-one Balloons*

1949 – Marguerite Henry – *King of the Wind*

1950 – Marguerite De Angeli – *The Door in the Wall*

1951 – Elizabeth Yates – *Amos Fortune, Free Man*

1952 – Eleanor Estes – *Ginger Pye*

1953 – Ann Nolan Clark – *Secret of the Andes*

1954 – Joseph Krumgold - *…And Now Miguel*

1955 – Meindert DeJong – *The Wheel on the School*

1956 – Jean Lee Latham – *Carry On, Mr. Bowditch*

1957 – Virginia Sorensen – *Miracles on Maple Hill*

1958 – Harold Keith – *Rifles for Watie*

1959 – Elizabeth George Speare – *The Witch of Blackbird Pond*

1960 – Joseph Krumgold – *Onion John*

1961 – Scott O'Dell – *Island of the Blue Dolphins*

1962 – Elizabeth George Speare – *The Bronze Bow*

1963 – Madeleine L'Engle – *A Wrinkle in Time*

1964 – Emily Neville – *It's Like This, Cat*

1965 – Maia Wojciechowska – *Shadow of a Bull*

1966 – Elizabeth Borton de Trevino – *I, Juan de Pareja*

1967 – Irene Hunt – *Up a Road Slowly*

1968 – Elaine Konigsburg – *From the Mixed-up Files of Mrs. Basil E. Frankweiler*

1969 – Lloyd Alexander – *The High King*

1970 – William H. Armstrong – *Sounder*

1971 – Betsy Byars – *Summer of the Swans*

1972 – Robert C. O'Brien – *Mrs. Frisby and the Rats of NIMH*
1973 – Jean Craighead George – *Julie of the Wolves*
1974 – Paula Fox – *The Slave Dancer*
1975 – Virginia Hamilton – *M.C. Higgins, the Great*
1976 – Susan Cooper – *The Grey King*
1977 – Mildred D. Taylor – *Roll of Thunder, Hear my Cry*
1978 – Katherine Paterson – *Bridge to Terabithia*
1979 – Ellen Raskin – *The Westing Game*
1980 – Joan W. Blos – *A Gathering of Days: A New England Girl's Journal, 1830-32*
1981 – Katherine Paterson – *Jacob Have I Loved*
1982 – Nancy Willard – *A Visit to William Blake's Inn: Poems for Innocent and Experienced Travelers*
1983 – Cynthia Voigt – *Dicey's Song*
1984 – Beverly Cleary – *Dear Mr. Henshaw*
1985 – Robin McKinley – *The Hero and the Crown*

1986 – Patricia MacLachlan – *Sarah, Plain and Tall*
1987 – Sid Fleischman – *The Whipping Boy*
1988 – Russell Freedman – *Lincoln: a Photobiography*
1989 – Paul Fleischman – *Joyful Noise: Poems for Two Voices*
1990 – Lois Lowry – *Number the Stars*
1991 – Jerry Spinelli – *Maniac Magee*
1992 – Phyllis Reynolds Naylor – *Shiloh*
1993 – Cynthia Rylant – *Missing May*
1994 – Lois Lowry – *The Giver*
1995 – Sharon Creech – *Walk Two Moons*
1996 – Karen Cushman – *The Midwife's Apprentice*
1997 – E.L. Konigsburg – *The View from Saturday*
1998 – Karen Hesse – *Out of the Dust*
1999 – Louis Sachar – *Holes*
2000 – Christopher Paul – *Bud, Not Buddy*
2001 – Richard Peck – *A Year Down Yonder*
2002 – Linda Sue Park – *A Single Shard*
2003 – Avi - *Crispin: The Cross of Lead*

CHRONOLOGY

1713 Born in Waltham, St. Lawrence, England on July 9
1730 Goes to Reading, gets a job at the *Mercury* newspaper
1737 Inherits part of William Carnan's estate
1738-39 Marries Mary Carnan
1740 Daughter Mary is born in March
1740 Sells haberdashery goods
1740 Publishes books in partnership with C. Micklewright
1740 Takes trip through parts of England
1741 Son John is born in September
1741 Operates printing business
1741 Sells "Blacking Ball" for shoes

1743 Son Francis is born on July 6th
1744 Opens a warehouse in London
1744 Publishes *A Little Pretty Pocket-Book*
1745 Moves to St. Paul's churchyard
1751 Publishes *The Lilliputian* magazine
1752 Son John dies
1764 Takes out a patent on an early version of a color printing press
1765 Publishes *The Renowned History of GILES GINGERBREAD* and *The Renowned History of Little GOODY TWO-SHOES*
1767 Dies on December 22

EVENTS IN JOHN NEWBERY'S LIFETIME

1706 *The Evening Post* becomes London's first evening newspaper.

1714 Fahrenheit temperature scale invented by Gabriel Fahrenheit.

1718 British astronomer Edmund Halley discovers that stars move, rather than staying still as had been previously believed.

1719 Daniel Defoe publishes *Robinson Crusoe.*

1721 Peter the Great becomes Emperor of Russia.

1726 Jonathan Swift publishes *Gulliver's Travels.*

1732 Benjamin Franklin publishes *Poor Richard's Almanack.*

1732 George Washington is born.

1735 John Adams, the second American President, is born.

1740 George Anson begins voyage around the world.

1742 Swedish astronomer Anders Celsius invents centigrade temperature scale.

1743 Thomas Jefferson, the third American President, is born.

1751 James Madison, the fourth American President, is born.

1752 Benjamin Franklin conducts his electricity experiments with a kite.

1754 French and Indian War between England and France in North America begins.

1755 Samuel Johnson publishes *Dictionary of the English Language.*

1760 George III becomes English king.

1762 Catherine the Great becomes Empress of Russia.

1764 London authorities develop house numbers.

1765 British Parliament passes the Stamp Act, which leads to the American Revolution.

1766 Oliver Goldsmith publishes novel *The Vicar of Wakefield.*

1775 Battles of Lexington and Concord begin American Revolution.

FURTHER RECOMMENDED READING

WORKS CONSULTED

Blackstock, Josephine. *Songs for Sixpence.* New York: Follett Publishing Company, 1955.

Picard, Liza. *Dr. Johnson's London.* New York: St. Martin's Press, 2001.

Townsend, John Rowe. *John Newbery and His Books.* Metuchen, NJ: The Scarecrow Press, Inc., 1994.

Welsh, Charles. *A Bookseller of the Last Century.* Clifton, NJ: Augustus M. Kelley, 1972.

INTERNET ADDRESSES

http://www.ala.org/alsc/newbery.html

http://www.bartleby.com/221/1611.html

http://www.iupui.edu/~engwft/newbery.htm

http://www.mothergoose.com/History/Newbery.htm

http://www.theatlantic.com/issues/1888jan/hewins.htm

INDEX